HURON COUNTY LIBRARY

WINGHAM BRANCH LIBRARY

O9-BRZ-556

Date Due

APR 28 1992		
May 29/92		
AUG 03 1993		
1993		
OCT 21		
NOV 5		
JUN 14		
JUL 14		
JAN 25		

BRODART, INC.   Cat. No. 23 233   Printed in U.S.A.

dy
e

4250

819   Nicholls, Sandra, 1956-
.154   The untidy bride / Sandra Nicholls. -- Kingston, Ont.
Nicho   : Quarry Press, c1991.
            68 p. -- (New Canadian poets series)

         06079962   ISBN:1550820214 (pbk.)

         I. Title

3444   92FEB17   06/wi   1-00571357

HURON COUNTY LIBRARY

NEW CANADIAN POETS SERIES

This series of titles from Quarry Press charts new directions being taken in contemporary Canadian poetry by presenting the first book-length work of innovative writers.

Other titles in the series include *Undressing the Dark* by Barbara Carey, *The Big Life Painting* by Ron Charach, *Stalin's Carnival* by Steven Heighton, and *The Speed of the Wheel Is Up to the Potter* by Sandy Shreve.

The Untidy Bride

Sandra Nicholls

Quarry Press

MAR 2 3 1992

4250

Copyright © Sandra Nicholls, 1991
All rights reserved.

The publisher thanks The Canada Council and the Ontario Arts Council for assistance in publishing this book.

Some of the poems in this book have appeared in *Anthos, Arc, Dandelion, Grain, Poetry Canada Review, Rideau Review, Room of One's Own,* and *Zymergy.* Several have been anthologized, in slightly different versions, in *Capital Poets,* published by Ouroborous Press.

The author would like to thank John Barton, Pier Giorgio Di Cicco, Nadine McInnis, Mary di Michele, Colin Morton, Robin Skelton and Jane Urquhart for their support and editorial guidance, as well as Blaine Marchand, Sue McMaster, Ronnie Brown, Chris Levenson, and the members of the Kingston Writing Workshops of 1988 and 1989 for their advice, their kindness, and their encouragement.

Canadian Cataloguing in Publication Data
  Nicholls, Sandra, 1956-
    The Untidy Bride
  (New Canadian poets series)
  Poems
  ISBN 1-55082-021-4
  I. Title. II. Series.
  PS8577.I185U68 1991   C811'.54   C91-090409-X
  PR9199.3.N43U68 1991

Cover art entitled ``Lady Magdalene (Dame Madeleine)'' by René Durocher, reproduced by permission Dr. Richard Guerrette. Photography by Don Whipple.

Design by Keith Abraham. Type imaging by Queen's University Imagesetting Services. Printed and bound in Canada by Hignell Printing, Winnipeg, Manitoba.

Published by **Quarry Press Inc.**, P.O. Box 1061, Kingston, Ontario K7L 4Y5 and P.O. Box 348, Clayton, New York 13624

This book is dedicated to my mum and dad, and to Rod.

Contents

THE UNTIDY BRIDE

WRITING ABOUT
THE DEAD

Writing About the Dead

When is it safe to write about the dead?
you have to make them welcome at first,
they're new at this, and insecure,
you might draw up a chair, pull out the albums,
you can even cry a little, if you want,
they go all soft at the sound of tears
forget their shyness, and stop by
you can comfort them with the quiet
scribbling of pens, the rustle of paper,
hunched over your desk at three a.m.
a time they particularly like,
feel their hands on your shoulders,
you expect them to be cold but they're warm,
they stay quiet until the last page,
just when you think you've got them right
they whisper in your ear
"was that how it really was?"

They laugh about the doubts
they've planted in your head,
you should hear the din
whenever the dead get together,
"did you see the look on her face?" they chortle,
until the tears come running down,
and then they tell each other how it was
for they never tire of the stories,
and they don't give a damn about accuracy,
they only ask to comfort themselves,
hoping they won't be forgotten.

Mid-Atlantic, 1955

This was how the ship prepared them:
tennis on the deck, ring and jack,
the sounds of carefree shipboard leisure,
first class travel, the false
floating bowl of artificial life,
my mother learns
a new vocabulary for distance,
fear, and failure, she has left everything
behind, she and my father in search
of the sheltering stranger, Montreal —
one thousand miles in from the open sea.

A child rocks in the bow of her womb,
knowing much better at sea how meaningless
time is, the bottomless hours, while days
on ships are marked for safety in hours:
tea in the afternoon, cocktails in the lounge
on a calm night, the brochure says,
but there are no calm nights, the sea
and the mohair collar sting her face,
he gave her that coat the day they left,
it cost him almost all he had; she holds
it close, a piece of good luck.

Why can't I see the horizon? she asks,
my father, having read the ship's log,
knows precisely that nothing
is impossible to measure. Here is a man
prepared to work for atomic energy.
He takes her hand and points,
eight miles away at fifty feet above
water, nearly ten at seventy five.
She nods, though she doesn't see
the steady line she wants to recognize.

Listen, he says, to the ship's whistle —
count the seconds between the sight of the steam
and the sound of the whistle, so precise,
one fifth of a mile for every second,
so easy to measure the distance between
where they are standing and other ships,
but she doesn't see another ship for days,
though once she spots a blue-white iceberg,
strange marker half-hidden under water.

My father handles every question,
can even tell her how to gauge
the ship's direction by pointing
the hour hand of her watch.
As she looks down she remembers
her own mother gave her the watch,
and she cannot see the numbers
or bisect the angle.

She longs to be going
in the same direction
as her husband, as the ship,
raises her head at last, hears
only the ship's whistle, far away,
voices rising from other decks,
and the turning, turning in her womb.

My Mother's Sister

You have a sister I've never met:
we never speak of her, the one who ran off
who had her baby in distant, noisy rooms
married young, and escaped the house
fleeing the grease and noise of domestic battle,
and leaving you behind.

I cling to the stories in pieces:
she refused to give you her bicycle,
was older and should have known better,
once threw a pair of scissors at you
the source of the anger has been forgotten
like family records gone missing, in the war,
in my mind the scene frozen like a photograph,
the scissors held in mid-air, blades swung open
by the force of the throw, for you another image:
the scissors lodged more than an inch
deep in the flesh of your thigh.

Eventually you hid the scar under your black stockings,
that was the year you worked at the factory
the country was up to its arms in war,
you met my father, he was wearing bottle green
the colour of gasmasks, the colour of the war,
the air turned yellow as distant bombs went down
on other houses, other prisons, but never yours,
the enemy seemed invincible, your father
standing at the top of the stairs
pointing at the clock, and loosening his belt.

Years later you shaped my childhood,
resolved to make it happier than yours
you told me, your only child,
the story of the scissors, and I claimed it
for my own. Only children, spoiled, they say.
No one sees the balled-up fist hidden
under the table, or the scissors we hurl
against the wall, the anger that finds no target,
falls inward, and draws no blood.

Fragile Souvenirs

1.

His beautiful wife:
she used to smash things.
He said it so quietly,
five years into the illness
the familiars of her life
became the enemy.

She wanted to move forward
quickly into death, wanted time
broken apart somehow,
how she hated these fragile souvenirs.

She couldn't break in,
objects were everywhere,
the crystal vase
bought in Vienna,
six glass camels, infuriating
perfect procession, the fuzzy
rind of dust everywhere
reminding her.

She smashed things looking
for a cool room, white
without furniture, where endings
could still be safely imagined.

2.

Everything's all right —
he says it so quietly.

As he reaches out now,
history filters
through an upturned bottle,
everything she hurls:
the years of glass
shatter

The Laws of Physics

My father's voice would blast
from a black box, the talking device
mounted on the wall
keeping us distant and safe,
while down in his workshop
he kept the company of his instruments:
boxes that glowed and beeped,
easily affected by pressure,
invisible changes in the atmosphere,
spare parts and transplants
from other machines,
tubes and levers like hearts
and tissue, wired in bundles.

When I stepped inside
it was like being in a room full of cats
with their ears pricked up,
next to the machines
I was dull and insensitive,
I understood nothing of physics,
or science, wanted only the comfort
of his solid fingers clasped
around mine, as he tried to explain
how sound waves travelled,
and we stood in awe before the green sky
of the oscilloscope screen, one voluptuous wave
skipping like a rope, and all around us
the restless, stuttering music
of the radio dials.

At night I stayed awake and listened
for messages on my father's radio receiver,
the loneliest of all words passing
through time and space, hopeful
dispatches fed into the empty night,
the imagined replies lost among the static.
I listened as the house filled
with electronic voices, the signals
of people far away, as into machines,
those like my father, poured their souls
into small black boxes, and those like me,
struggled in silence, with science and codes.

Glass Lanterns

In the dream time
my father was dying,
and I was fighting
a private civil war.

And now,
wherever I am
the guns are pointed,
ready to quiet my deaths.

Ice has formed
outside the window;
the sound of glass,
lanterns in the wind.

We all hear the crash
a crack, and then a violent
pull, the curtains rent
wide to the night,
each of us wrenched awake
from our secret, separate journeys,
father, mother, me.

A glass branch
has split the window;
two weeks, the doctors say,
and only my father, dying,
regrets the knowledge
of spring huddled
under ground.

Illness in the Family

Returning from the hospital
I see my mother standing
at the window, waiting
in the way of all women.

I have delivered the silk
flowers, the ones we bought
for my father, knowing
they would last.

My mother turns from the window,
flowers are very efficient, she says,
but they come and go.

Women bury whole lives waiting,
for lovers to call,
for doctors to drive
their slow, straight needles
into patient spines.

I suppose we are all waiting;
even in that room
flowers crouch in a window
trying to burst into flame.

The King of Paper Cups

how dare you lie there
tubes up your nose
unable to speak
something in my throat
speaks from memory
I press my face down
close beside you,
all I would have said is piling up.

> *Can you hear me through the plastic vines?*
> *time here is something else   like at the zoo*
> *they measure it in feedings, pills and operations*
> *they call me the king of paper cups*
> *why don't you eat one of those chocolates?*
> *beside me on the metallic table. I know you're there.*

did you give way before I could
negotiate traffic stops and elevators
and schedules and hurl myself across
the country: I will you to wake up
to deny everything.

> *I hear you moving a white rustle of sheets*
> *like paper   your breathing   at my mouth in my face*

Something like silence
claimed you for its own
before I could reach you.
Don't make me walk
alone down that corridor.

> *I know everything about the corridor*
> *the yellow arrows   all I know is through the door*
> *white bodies pass and vines and fluids*
> *I watch the clock   my blood hangs   in a glass bottle*
> *above my head, an enclosed wound.*

I wonder from what place
you hear me calling.

> *I see you frown see the doctors frown from behind their*
> *charts guardians of secrets times I escape behind the*
> *white curtain.*

My God, that man
in the next bed moaning.

> *When the lights go out*
> *I watch the orderlies in their green caps. Night*
> *here never really comes there is   always a light*
> *somwhere.*

I wonder from what place,
father, you hear me calling.

> *I long to tell*
> *from the other side:*
> *the sound of thin paper*
> *a white rustle*
> *the breath of flowers.*

Grief

We stepped silently
into the blue shadows;
whatever was left
of our conversation
remained behind us,
forgotten excitement
at the start of flame
we watched the fever
of the streetlamp,
its final tremor
casting the street
into yellow darkness.
And each of our lives
being just that fragile,
we lit matches
trembling in the doorway.
I could not bear
the quick terrible movement
of your expert hands,
or the sound that rose
from the pavement,
the spent match folding inward,
my father alone falling into light.

The Days Like Braille

after her husband dies she begins
lengthening time into ropes, ropes
into swords, the house is littered
with the small executions of her days

her fingers move from morning across
the days like braille, she recognizes
the shapes and codes of familiar hours
their punctuations: coffee at ten, the twelve
o'clock news, the sound of the postman
the long scream that is afternoon widening,
one hour's passage dissolving into the next

but today a bird, one wing crippled
drops from the fence to her garden
as she steps outside to offer comfort
the hours narrow into thin needles of light
mending the wound of the afternoon,
the air still hot with the panic of wings

Solace

I can tell by the curve
of your body, the way
it curves apart
from my hand,
that you find my timing
inappropriate.

But grief makes the body
greedy for pleasure,
as if death could be held
at the door, with a sigh.

And now, as your body
turns away, declares
one of us coward,
I must lean, undisturbed
into my grief, I must never
betray my sorrow.

My Father's Ashes

I entered the forest
arms laden with lilac
and my father's ashes,
seeds from another time.

The full-blown forest
thick with rain,
the dark heavy branches
and the rising river.

Golden eyes watched us
from the hollows
as we scattered the ashes,
none of us knowing what to say.

The rain-soaked blossoms
fell from my hands.
This was my father's
sacred place, heavy and dark.

And even now,
on certain rainy days the sudden
scent of lilac can fill the forest
with his unending grace.

Bellevue Garden, Kingston
(for Bronwen Wallace)

Mysterious, what goes on
underground, where the garden
groans under a mottled sky;
familiar scraping din of shovel,
sour leaves cramped in a barrow
thick with discarded root, plunder
of gardens that began before.

Underground, plans are unfolding
you can hear the black soil sketching
marrow, marigolds, poppies,
you brought me here to listen. Listen —
in the leaves of the ornamental corn
sudden flight of birds.

We have been talking
as women will, and have before,
marking the impressions of our names,
an old wooden bucket sighs, half-filled
with rain, pumpkins begin under the ground
in small mounds. In the earth, imprints
of leaves: time and her notebooks. We are drawn
to the darkest part of the garden
and move among the fallen apples
quietly re-designing themselves
for the journey home.

Born Again

You'll be born again at the seaside,
blue-striped pavillions and candy
wrappers, perambulators and girls
with popcorn curls and parasols.

Or in a northern country
scalloped in ice, landscape
of icebergs, where half the life
is underwater. Being invisible.

At least somewhere foreign
to the dark skirts of memory
rustling and tugging on the old ground
where the questions arose
and the answers began to slip away,
where you traced the migration of your first blood,
and lost your place
to someone who cleared his throat
found himself called a man,
and later: husband, father.

In unnamed places memory unfurls,
the smoke rising out of fires
to be shaped, altered, plundered
as you wish, finally you have the time
to re-create your geography
and it's God's last laugh:
you come back as yourself —
all your regrets intact.

ACCURACIES

Changing Lanes

You're about to pull over:
something large and moving quickly
appears in the corner of your eye,
lurching back you resolve
to remember the sudden beacon
of green light ahead
and closer, on the icy window
fern rivers and maps of frost,
the small blue veins that spill
across your hands
suddenly bound to the wheel,
and like an instant photograph:
appearing from darkness,
your own daughter, sleepy face frozen
in the rear-view mirror, you have
to turn your head and look,
convince yourself she is really there.

The house you left behind is empty
will the telephone start to ring?
always the call that comes so
unexpected, and no one there
to answer: someone moves
too fast, too far, without looking —
nothing is more important now
than making a space to see
what you missed before.

Every time you thought your hands held
tight to the wheel, they were sliding off,
living wasn't meant to be made easy,
when your father was dying you arranged
for happy things, to ease the pain,
the small and awful injuries:
cutting a piece of meat for a man
too weak to hold the knife,
and when you thought the road was clear
something blurred went spinning past
you thought you saw your mother,
long since gone, so far away
you could only just make her out
as she swerved by, someone passing
in the corridor, a patient whose face
you can't even see, the light goes
so fast, you have the feeling you're probably
crazy, your father winks and then
he's gone, perhaps you imagined it
only seconds passed but somehow
it was your whole life in there,
you can't even remember the name
of the dog you loved in Grade Two,
the one killed by a speeding car
moving too fast, no one saw.

Frost builds on the windscreen
you can't see in or out,
there are no details, just a blur:
the speedometer races ahead —
sixty — seventy — eighty —
no fixed point to the miles,
the needle frantic at the speed
where your heart would stop —
only there you are, staring ahead,
shouting in the language of broken glass —
the faces in the mirrors and the photographs
dissolving backwards into dark pools
the round plates of light extending and retracting
hurling backwards through your life,
a bright streak of time, spinning mid-air.

Birth

When I was born
mother was dreaming
inner palms and tropical water
tunnelled prayers

father was dreaming
banks and theories
endless construction

I was born in this swell
cymbals and sounds
inside waves turning me
inside out, mother was there
and father, I saw a stranger
reflected in their eyes,
wearing my skin
the wrong way round
I came apart in panic
I was drowning
a jangle of instruments
rushed at my ears
the doctor's hands
were made of steel.

After it was over,
I lay in the light
with the other babies
we plotted together
ways to begin
making the passage
home.

Small Cracks

Mother sings me lullabies from small
places where the seam pulls
quietly apart; a spine of thread
joining one half to the other
small cracks in the mended
china, turned to face right side
round on the shelf.

The woman who taught me
these tight melodies
has so many disguises
she could slide between
you and your lover
and never be seen.

I hear her singing
between the threads
of my clothes, a melody
bursts from the place
where your hand touches
my cheek, and as I begin
to cross the blank
pages with words, the notes
rise between the blade
and the exposed bone.

Mother

The tap picks five a.m. to begin
its steady dripping, the hammers
of morning are pressed to the window
she curls away from the dawn
her eyes half-closed, her child asleep
in another house, in another part of town.

It's the time when she feels the weight
of her blood, when the sun moves slowly,
heavy with unfinished night, the time
she reveals her age to herself, the years
that gathered their arrows and fired in silence
while she slept unaware of the danger.

She remembers the man who slept beside her
through so many nights, the man whose ears
were tuned with hers to listen for a voice
crying at the door, her child awake
filled with fear, alone in the hall
five a.m. nightmares pinned to her eyes.

Diana at the Loom

Let's have lunch, she says,
bearing in mind the meeting
at two, the nanny at four,
the husband at six,
the pillars of revolution
hang from her wrists
as she tries to eat, eyes
her watch and looks forward
in the wrong direction.

She tells me she is trying
to grow a second self
from the inside out, and
imagines the skeleton forming
a new family of bones,
she tells me
of the crowded conditions
under her skin, the unfamiliar
alphabet of division
without space.

At night
she hears the sound
of ancient women dancing
on the skins of her
discarded selves, a rabid
dance of upturned mythology,
in her ears a tumble
of stones, their history
gathered in empty places.

She hears them pounding
at night, in her brain,
Diana on fire before the loom
and Athena, restless at the wheel.

Modern Woman

That time of month is here again,
across the breakfast table I lumber for the salt,
am wedged tight into my chair
hair a sticky mess
my fat fingers smudged in marmalade.

Eventually I rise,
large and woman-heavy,
carry my plate and knife
to the white kitchen
pour coffee; a mistake, I know,
and even my breath spreads thick and dark
in the swollen breath
of the first morning.

I'd prefer to wear a blanket,
a large hat, and slippers.
But I remember,
I am a modern woman.
When that time comes along
the modern woman takes up sports
goes swimming
rides horses.

So I squeeze my skin into the shape of my clothes,
press my feet into shoes
designed for infertile women,
shuffle cumbersome on to the street,
carry what feels like the weight of the sea
in my thighs.

I spend the day avoiding mirrors, and
women on horseback.

Traces of Faith

On good days, God
is a crazy vision,
bad-tempered,
he parades around
in my head
wearing flimsy pajamas,
threatening to pull the strings
and disappear.

On good days God
camps out in seashells
makes noises like waves,
the ears of my children
are filled with his breathing.

Whenever I can
I picture him shrouded
in a cloud of light
shot with transparent veins,
pale as a glass marble.

When I can't sleep,
he is darkness cornered
behind my eyes,
an invisible mirror.
He wakes me with voices:
skeleton children
speaking in tongues.

These visions appear
on good days. Most of the time,
in the place of faith,
I plunder the garden,
looking for traces,
footprints.

Losing the Baby

Scientists claim the egg they found
was the size of a human head —

imagine two thousand years of lying
dormant, imagine the shell
remaining a shell
an outline filled with air,
they were looking for an embryo;
the chance to start again,
but all that caught
in the scanner's eye
was dust.

They should have been looking for ghosts:
the things inside that never settle
not in two thousand years
not in a lifetime.

Holding Back

I handle babies carefully,
being unfamiliar;
this does not mean
that I love less, though awkwardly
I come with my offerings,
a mantle of wishes,
and the right intentions.

Have I come too late or
was I never welcome here,
in your exclusive motherhood?

You hold back
discoveries, the first this
and the first that,
and let us first dissect
every world problem,
talk of anything but babies;
can this creation be so hard?

Above us the moon rises
like a fist; the baby cries,
I have no children;
you ask me nothing.

I feel myself dividing,
twice removed
from an entire universe.

Elevator

On the elevator door, large, scary
print of a boot, a violence
barely hidden, left by a man
who works in the building
when the halls are quiet, at night.

Caught behind this door
which won't push open,
refusing to yield to his touch,
he strikes out in the half-light:
the bleak emergency of after dark.

He must be a lonely man,
for the heart can act like this,
an elevator door
that leaves you imprisoned
between two floors.

Like that first time, pried loose
from his mother's thighs
into antiseptic daylight,
stamping his rage
the length of that passage,
at the first betrayal.

Love's first touch was cold as steel,
the forceps denied him, even then,
the gentle easing of a human hand,
into the distant light.

Earth Apnea

This habit of sleeping
slackens my grip on a world
which never closes, daylight stays open
the neon limbs of the cities
feeling the pressure to be on.
Sleep is for the weak,
so I keep moving, all-night prayer,
late night television, no need
to shut down. If we could only
turn and see ourselves
disappearing,
like the photographs
that don't turn out of the places
we may never see again.

Climates turn themselves inside out.
We laugh. We keep babies
the size of thumbs alive, and withhold death
from the sick, no one's going to cheat us
of our time.
We turn our backs on the sun
falling asleep at the controls,
the surgeon working for 36 hours
closes his eyes and it's over
in seconds, in the guts
of nuclear plants, workers are drowsy,
we've even made plans for the end of the world,
books on civil defence prepare us,
imagine haemorrhaging with the desire
to use up what's left,
we'll need tranquilisers to cope,
hoping that someone will find us in time,
pull us out, pay attention —
while the earth dreams
of putting her head in a chamber filled
with gas, wanting only to lie down
in a darkened room, to be quiet for a while.

Becoming Dangerous

She is learning to find herself in the dark
pools at the edges of the alphabet
hunting wild birds that rise and scatter
the scrub trembling behind them
she learned in the past to creep
and be quiet, silence the flapping of wings,
but now she's becoming dangerous: the words cling
like stained feathers to her lips.

Once he wanted a cross
big enough to fill his bed,
a woman small enough
to wear on a chain.

How she longs to make flesh
of his words, to hunt them down,
hang their small, bleached skeletons
from around her neck. She begins to howl,
as she pulls the sharpened
bone from her side,
she already knows she must throw it
to the ground and begin
all over again.

THE
UNTIDY BRIDE

The Male Feminist

Beware the male
feminist, suddenly welcome
in a wary circle
of women.

He is more than
the new man,
he has crossed over
he is in tight
he loves us all,
the same.

Delving into our
alphabet, he would have us
forget all our stories
and his.

This is the man who wants
you to feel free
about your body,
but only with him.
Oh, but he loves
all women.

This is the man
who wants you to feel
good about those imperfect parts
you never considered, until now,
the man so bent on loving you best
that you can't relax,
the man who watches
to see if your eyelids flutter.

Go out and find an ill-tempered man,
one who is lonely and tired of loving,
a man trapped at the edge of the world,
a man who would take you inside his head
down unchecked forests, where you might falter
and not be praised.

Casualties

We have been
in artificial light,
the intimacy of strangers
in the cinema,
the wax candle darkness
of a café.

We have unwound
our emergencies,
unravelled our wounds:
scarred warriors
sewn together
for an evening.

All the night
you read to me,
and unable to say everything
I say nothing, in the silence:
a thousand quiet accidents.

All the night
I shift my wounds,
to cope with your embrace.

Metamorphosis

You take me, thrumming
up the stairs to a room
where you practise loving,
between us the air
is black and blue
with our kisses.

Your old victims rise
from the bed;
my knees begin to tremble
I cannot keep
myself from their eyes
or quiet the sound
of my ridiculous breathing.

I place myself white
in your hands, peel back
my lizard skin
offer my green caress;
my kisses breed and sting
and circle in swarms;
my arms grow
poisonous leaves.

Together in the dark
our blood grows warm,
we blunder
in the blackness
while love, fooled once more
bursts angry
from the deepening shadows.

Sleeping Under Glass

Reading in bed is a love
that we don't share,
I've learned to fall asleep
in the glare of the lamp
learned to enter darkness
by 60 watts of light.

I sometimes wonder
if you close your eyes at all
if you spend those restless hours
trying to understand:

you'd like to get inside
measure it out, poke around,
prod the soft centre,
turn on your flashlight,
perhaps take a few scrapings
to examine later;
see if you might recognize
something, a plant or a photograph,
you want to know
while lying beside me
how it was being apart
from you, all that time,
knowing I'm unable to tell you
in the morning, where I've been.

did you think
as you wandered
tunnel after tunnel,
there might be initials
carved on bark, a train
derailed, a few explosions,
some broken teeth?

no, what you're hoping
you'll find and expect to see
under the glass and in the bright
glare of the lamp is a trace
of yourself.

maybe sleep is a kind of ending,
rehearsing for something more
than a retraceable escape. I wonder
if you know, when I close
my eyes at night
it's a little like dying:
and death is always careful,
locks the door from behind.

Breaking Up

This morning only your clothes,
your jeans turned outwards with the memory of knees,
the pale islands, their fragrance so familiar
beneath the arms of your shirt, same shirt worn soft
from running, sweating, loving
thin where it stretched across your back
when your arms bent their way around me,
your socks curled and clustered
across the carpet, and under the bed.

Still crazy to love your clothes;
how they call up the shape of your body
the unhurried way they hang in the closet,
sure of your return, the way they invite me
to climb inside. The way there is always room.

Poisoned

Three days ago he left.
She didn't know how much
or how long it would take,
she chose silence, deadly poison,
the house too quiet; she lies awake
gripped to one side of the bed
listening for sounds, inventing rustlings
rattle of footsteps or doors that slam,
while a mouse moves through the hidden arteries
of the house, trying not to lose itself,
sightless now, half-stumbling
well-travelled tunnels that twist suddenly,
three days of treason in its blood.

Her lover came back for his things,
no longer seeing
her or the sheet of sleepless nights
she wore wrapped around her body,
he laughed at her inept attempts:
the toxic seeds
she spread along its trail.

She watched his hands as they set
and released the trap he claimed
brought on the inevitable, and fast.
Watched as he mangled bait
on steel teeth, watched his fingers
as they guided trap to ledge
gently as breathing, watched
and remembered his touch.

Twenty minutes he'd said,
but days went by
finally a snap
slapped the air
in the kitchen, and she froze
then what she didn't expect:
a frantic sound like a child
hammering again and again
at a toy.

She hoped it would die
out of sight, never imagined the grief.
The eyes
rammed to the edges of their sockets,
small body a crooked hook.

Now love's gone quiet,
she buried it whole,
still caught in the trap,
eyes wide open.

Married Man

Being with you that month, he says,
was a denial of who I am, of everyone
who is near and dear, of all that I love,
across the table he expects me
to think better of him, allow him some grace
at my expense, tossed like scrap
on the heap of those not near
or dear, and for this he wants
some sort of tribute,
even understanding, and I am again
dumbfounded at the way some men
rationalize their own folly.
Seeing the look on my face
he quickly tries to recover and says
"the sex was great, of course."

Memory

Careful —
where you walk, last year
a disappearance, there by the door
a mutilation, and there are fewer
and fewer places you can recall,
the weight always rushes
straight down so you wear
your head lightly, loose
above all this commotion,
it murmurs to you:
I am only a few ounces
of matter and sponge.

You wake up forgetting,
move across the floor:
nothing is clear, you can't
settle anywhere, your head
dangles loose and uneasy,
so light it slips
between the cracks,
and only some water,
a few white bones and
a small red heart
remember you were here at all.

Mapmaking

1.

My first day married —
you at the wheel of our rented car,
I the keeper of the map
holding it upside down so I can see
what's right side up
the map aligns itself to the eyes, to the road,
I am looking for turns and thinking
of those Russian cartographers who finally admitted
they misdrew the maps deliberately for years
so that landmarks and rivers
didn't show up where you expected them to,
and the country was only known to those
who knew the country anyway. I am just about to tell you
the exit is to the left when you turn
and frown, tell me I am holding
the map the wrong way up and frankly
it looks right to me, so I ignore this
and carry on. This is where we have
our first fight.

2.

That first kiss when you drew back
the soft centre of your mouth from mine
you walked back down the aisle
with someone else.

3.

While all the guests were dreaming dreamy
thoughts at home while you were pouring
champagne into the glasses in the kitchen
of our suite, I put the wedding dress back on
and waited, in my newly-married skin,
buried under lace, under wanting.

But when you came into the room,
you made me save the dress
only the rustle in the silence
as I stuffed the lace and satin
into the plastic clothing bag
I was thinking about *The Big Chill*
the opening scene, the body,
I zipped up the bag.

4.

This is how it begins, the being
responsible for everything
banging your head and finding yourself
apologizing to the cupboard.
Here is my apology to the clerk at the inn,
to the man in the restaurant, to everyone
who noticed we just got married, the wedding bands
were so bright it was unnatural. Here's my apology to all those
who came to the wedding, to the organ player,
to my parents, to all the people I'm disappointing.
The veil dropped silently in the night,
I would like to replace my heart
with something more reliable and oh yes, I apologize
for not giving in right away, for keeping the apology to myself
for not seeing that I was disappointed too
and here is my apology to the cake —
to the goddamn cake — which I swallowed whole,
and here is my apology to an idea too delicate to hold.
and finally, here is my apology to myself,
which wasn't included
in any of the wedding arrangements.

5.

I've always wanted a round room
no edges, corners or straight lines
we cross over to an island
on our honeymoon journey
there is so much rain the landscape disappears
I can't resist the urge to tell you
I've guided us safely
I've brought us here.

The houses are lit like monuments,
paper cutouts face flat to the twisted road and the inn
we booked has a white piano and an art gallery and people
speaking softly I love it already I can smell the sea
in the sheets of the four poster bed
the first thing I want when I see that bed is to climb up
and make love but you're busy in the corner folding
the map which I have creased in all the wrong places
I see the way your jaw is set
and I don't say anything and I see from the bed the map closing
on all the rivers and countries.

A Fog in Victoria

Coming from another city. This gray, waving wall needs a new name, not one I've uprooted from another place. On the table is the book you gave me, before I left. A gray wind blows in and lifts open the pages. There you are. A scroll of good intent. The way love always starts.

The book falls open with a familiar sigh, shaped in the past tense. You were always so cryptic and clever in love. You followed me through unnamed climates, my heart was a broken compass you spun round in your hands. The room is quiet. I fold the book to my chest, listen for your voice.

There is only the fog. And breathing I am unable to name.

Magnetism

The distance between the yellow leaf
resting on the shoulder of your blue shirt
and my hand resting beside you on the wooden bench:
the space of time held in a breath. I want
to brush it away but I haven't touched you,
nothing so simple
and invisible between us yet.

I imagine the leaf rising
and falling as you breathe,
we stare beyond the river, our words
pulled by the wind as it lifts
the fine hairs on your arms.

We are held as the earth holds,
fixed between two poles,
we are magnets learning
to be roused by reaching,
I do not touch you
or move away, we suspend
the power that can lift
steel, split the world in two.

Love Poem

How close you hold your guitar,
its warm, luminous body in the light,
as your fingers call up the gentle
memory of the music, your eyes half-close,
and sitting together on the edge of the bed
we have seldom been closer,
when the songs cease, I touch your skin
the longing of one for the other
reconciled, my hands follow the falling
music the length of your spine,
our bodies balanced over the pulse
of an older song, I pass my lips,
my hands, over your eyes, your mouth,
as one stray note descending
catches its graceful wing
at the heart's edge, floats
into the chamber and finds
within itself, an inevitable music.

The Untidy Bride

welcome her in, the untidy bride,
how carefully she has arranged
the many faces of her bad days,
the entanglements trailing behind
sprung from every ill-timed hope.

welcome this bride, she has been
scrubbed and scraped clean: that mess
where she clung to her life, scoured raw,
the disappointments packed together
like earth jammed under her fingernails,
and past pleasures concealed: a softness
behind the ears. But it makes no difference,
we need another chance to begin:
all this whiteness, these wedding vows,
like so many times before, the start
of school, fresh pencils, their points sharp
as diamonds, the blankets of white
paper disguise our fear, we are about
to be altered, we must make ready.

Each time we are a new combination,
a practical weave of the old fibres
of the other lives, yet we bind
the bride in sheet-white folds
and glitter to disguise her disarray,
though as she walks before her past
to the future, with every turn of her head
those untidy signals of memory, doubt,
a thread begins to unravel, a film
of dust falling like a veil
in the rooms of a house
she hasn't entered.